WAR

HAROLD PINTER

WAR

faber and faber

First published in 2003
by Faber and Faber Limited
3 Queen Square London WC1N 3AU

Typeset by Faber and Faber
Printed in England by Character Print and Design Ltd

A CIP record for this book
is available from the British Library
ISBN 0–571–22131–9

2 4 6 8 10 9 7 5 3 1

Acknowledgements

'Meeting' first published in the *Guardian*, 28 August 2002, copyright © 2002, Harold Pinter; 'After Lunch' first published in the *Guardian*, 5 October 2002, copyright © 2002, Harold Pinter; 'God Bless America' first published in the *Guardian*, 22 January 2003, copyright © 2003, Harold Pinter; 'The Bombs', first published in the *Independent*, 15 February 2003, copyright © 2003, Harold Pinter; 'Democracy' first published in the *Spectator*, 15 March 2003, copyright © 2003, Harold Pinter; 'Weather Forecast', first published in the *Guardian*, 20 March 2003, copyright © 2003, Harold Pinter; Turin Speech first published in the *Daily Telegraph*, 11 December 2002, copyright © 2002, Harold Pinter; 'American Football' first published in the *Socialist*, 15–28 January 1992, copyright © 1992, Harold Pinter; 'Death' first published in the *Times Literary Supplement*, 10 October 1997, copyright © 1997, Harold Pinter.

Contents

Meeting

It is the dead of night

The long dead look out towards
The new dead
Walking towards them

There is a soft heartbeat
As the dead embrace
Those who are long dead
And those of the new dead
Walking towards them

They cry and they kiss
As they meet again
For the first and last time

August 2002

After Lunch

And after noon the well-dressed creatures come
To sniff among the dead
And have their lunch

And all the many well-dressed creatures pluck
The swollen avocados from the dust
And stir the minestrone with stray bones

And after lunch
They loll and lounge about
Decanting claret in convenient skulls

September 2002

God Bless America

Here they go again,
The Yanks in their armoured parade
Chanting their ballads of joy
As they gallop across the big world
Praising America's God.

The gutters are clogged with the dead
The ones who couldn't join in
The others refusing to sing
The ones who are losing their voice
The ones who've forgotten the tune.

The riders have whips which cut.
Your head rolls onto the sand
Your head is a pool in the dirt
Your head is a stain in the dust
Your eyes have gone out and your nose
Sniffs only the pong of the dead
And all the dead air is alive
With the smell of America's God.

January 2003

The Bombs

There are no more words to be said
All we have left are the bombs
Which burst out of our head
All that is left are the bombs
Which suck out the last of our blood
All we have left are the bombs
Which polish the skulls of the dead

February 2003

Democracy

There's no escape.
The big pricks are out.
They'll fuck everything in sight.
Watch your back.

March 2003

Weather Forecast

The day will get off to a cloudy start.
It will be quite chilly
But as the day progresses
The sun will come out
And the afternoon will be dry and warm.

In the evening the moon will shine
And be quite bright.
There will be, it has to be said,
A brisk wind
But it will die out by midnight.
Nothing further will happen.

This is the last forecast.

March 2003

Turin Speech

On the occasion of the award of an Honorary Degree
27 November 2002

Earlier this year I had a major operation for cancer. The operation and its after-effects were something of a nightmare. I felt I was a man unable to swim bobbing about under water in a deep dark endless ocean. But I did not drown and I am very glad to be alive. However, I found that to emerge from a personal nightmare was to enter an infinitely more pervasive public nightmare – the nightmare of American hysteria, ignorance, arrogance, stupidity and belligerence: the most powerful nation the world has ever known effectively waging war against the rest of the world. 'If you are not with us you are against us,' President Bush has said. He has also said, 'We will not allow the world's worst weapons to remain in the hands of the world's worst leaders.' Quite right. Look in the mirror, chum. That's you.

The US is at this moment developing advanced systems of 'weapons of mass destruction' and is prepared to use them where it sees fit. It has more of them than the rest of the world put together. It has walked away from international agreements on biological and chemical weapons, refusing to allow inspection of its own factories. The hypocrisy behind its public declarations and its own actions is almost a joke.

The United States believes that the three thousand deaths in New York are the only deaths that count, the only deaths that matter. They are American deaths. Other deaths are unreal, abstract, of no consequence.

The three thousand deaths in Afghanistan are never referred to.

The hundreds of thousands of Iraqi children dead through US and British sanctions which have deprived them of essential medicines are never referred to.

The effect of depleted uranium, used by America in the Gulf War, is never referred to. Radiation levels in Iraq are appallingly high. Babies are born with no brain, no eyes, no genitals. Where they do have ears, mouths or rectums, all that issues from these orifices is blood.

The two hundred thousand deaths in East Timor in 1975 brought about by the Indonesian government but inspired and supported by the United States are never referred to.

The half a million deaths in Guatemala, Chile, El Salvador, Nicaragua, Uruguay, Argentina and Haiti, in actions supported and subsidised by the United States, are never referred to.

The millions of deaths in Vietnam, Laos and Cambodia are no longer referred to.

The desperate plight of the Palestinian people, the central factor in world unrest, is hardly referred to.

But what a misjudgement of the present and what a misreading of history this is.

People do not forget. They do not forget the death of their fellows, they do not forget torture and mutilation, they do not forget injustice, they do not forget oppression, they do not forget the terrorism of mighty powers. They not only don't forget. They strike back.

The atrocity in New York was predictable and inevitable. It was an act of retaliation against constant and systematic manifestations of state terrorism on the part of the United States over many years, in all parts of the world.

In Britain the public is now being warned to be 'vigilant' in preparation for potential terrorist acts. The language is in itself preposterous. How will – or can – public vigilance be embodied? Wearing a scarf over your mouth to keep out poison gas? However, terrorist attacks are quite likely, the inevitable result of our Prime Minister's contemptible and shameful subservience to the United States. Apparently a terrorist poison gas attack on the London Underground system was recently prevented. But such an act may indeed take place. Thousands of schoolchildren travel on the London Underground every day. If there is a poison gas attack from which they die, the responsibility will rest entirely on the shoulders of our Prime Minister. Needless to say, the Prime Minister does not travel on the Underground himself.

The planned war against Iraq is in fact a plan for premeditated murder of thousands of civilians in order, apparently, to rescue them from their dictator.

The United States and Britain are pursuing a course which can lead only to an escalation of violence throughout the world and finally to catastrophe.

It is obvious, however, that the United States is bursting at the seams to attack Iraq. I believe that it will do this – not just to take control of Iraqi oil – but because the US administration is now a bloodthirsty wild animal. Bombs are its only vocabulary. Many Americans, we know, are horrified by the posture of their government but seem to be helpless.

Unless Europe finds the solidarity, intelligence, courage and will to challenge and resist US power Europe itself will deserve Alexander Herzen's definition: 'We are not the doctors. We are the disease.'

American Football
A reflection upon the Gulf War

Hallelujah!
It works.
We blew the shit out of them.

We blew the shit right back up their own ass
And out their fucking ears.

It works.
We blew the shit out of them.
They suffocated in their own shit!

Hallelujah.
Praise the Lord for all good things.

We blew them into fucking shit.
They are eating it.

Praise the Lord for all good things.

We blew their balls into shards of dust,
Into shards of fucking dust.

We did it.

Now I want you to come over here and kiss me
    on the mouth.

August 1991

Death

Where was the dead body found?
Who found the dead body?
Was the dead body dead when found?
How was the dead body found?

Who was the dead body?

Who was the father or daughter or brother
Or uncle or sister or mother or son
Of the dead and abandoned body?

Was the body dead when abandoned?
Was the body abandoned?
By whom had it been abandoned?

Was the dead body naked or dressed for a journey?

What made you declare the dead body dead?
Did you declare the dead body dead?
How well did you know the dead body?
How did you know the dead body was dead?

Did you wash the dead body
Did you close both its eyes
Did you bury the body
Did you leave it abandoned
Did you kiss the dead body